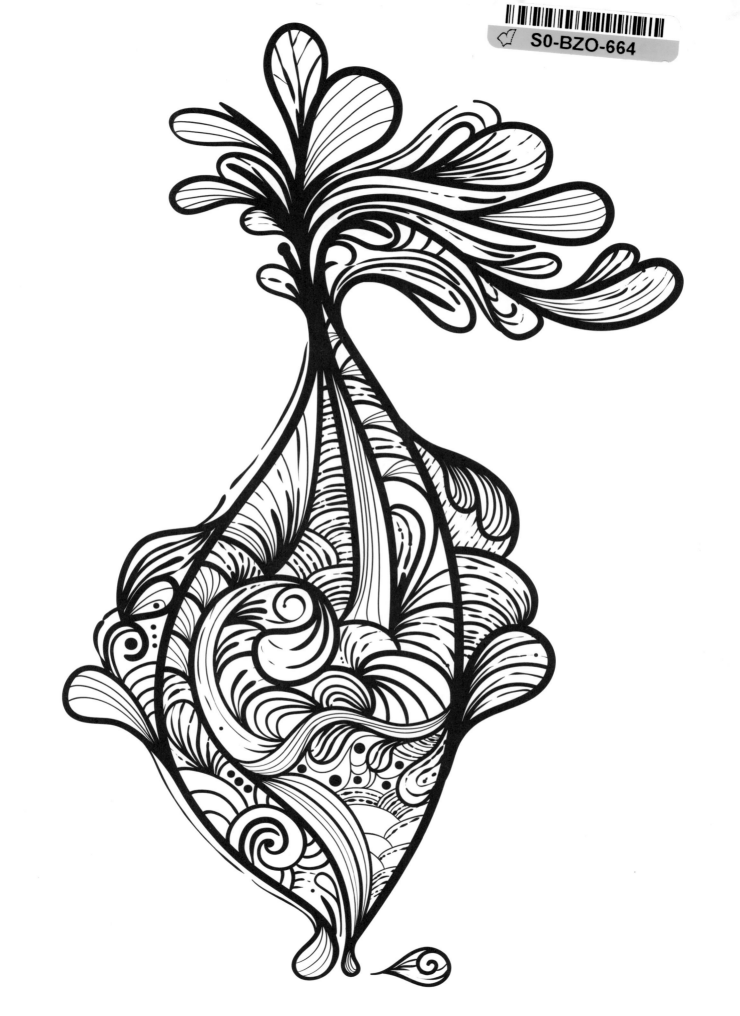

# Life Aquatic

## An Adult Coloring Book

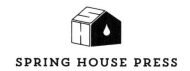

SPRING HOUSE PRESS

Published by:
Spring House Press
3613 Brush Hill Court
Nashville, TN 37216

ISBN: 978-1-940611-51-8
Printed in the United States of America
First Printing: April 2016

To learn more about Spring House Press books
or to find a retailer near you,
email info@springhousepress.com
or visit us at: www.springhousepress.com.

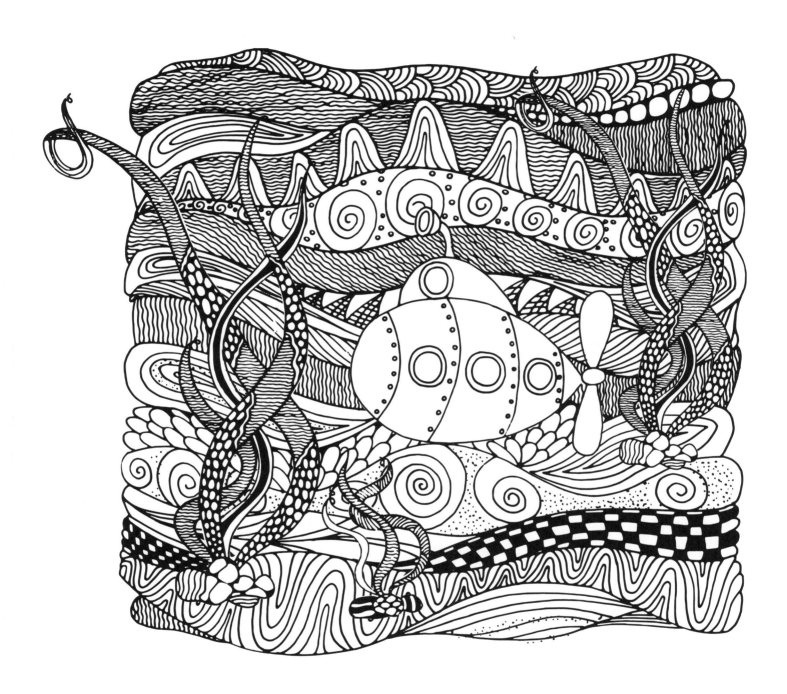

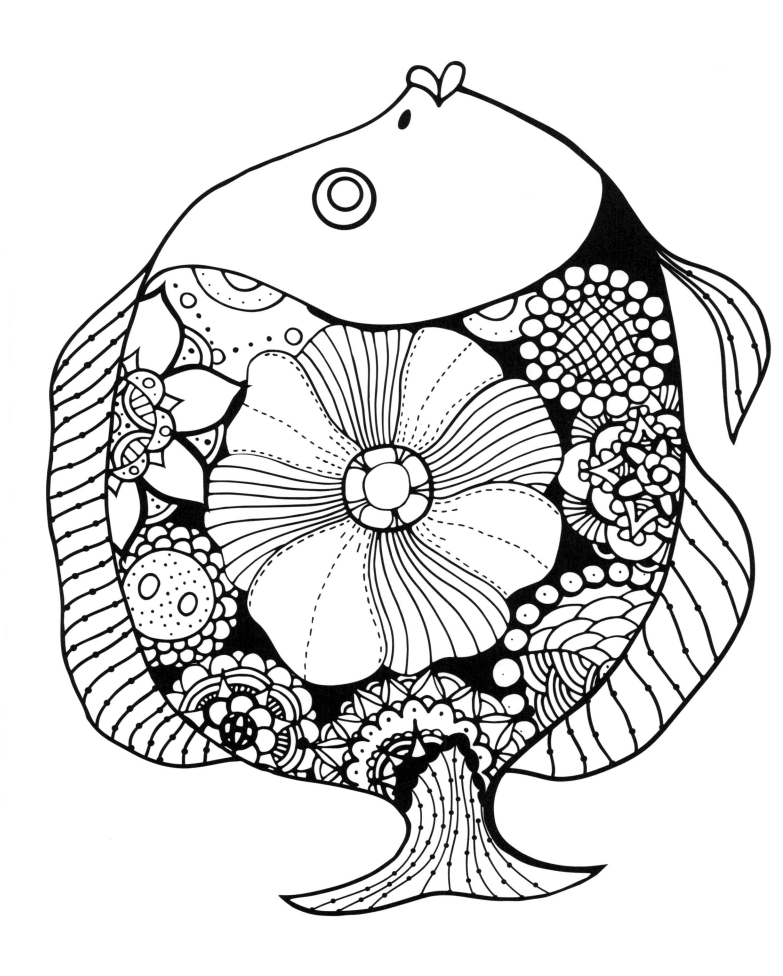

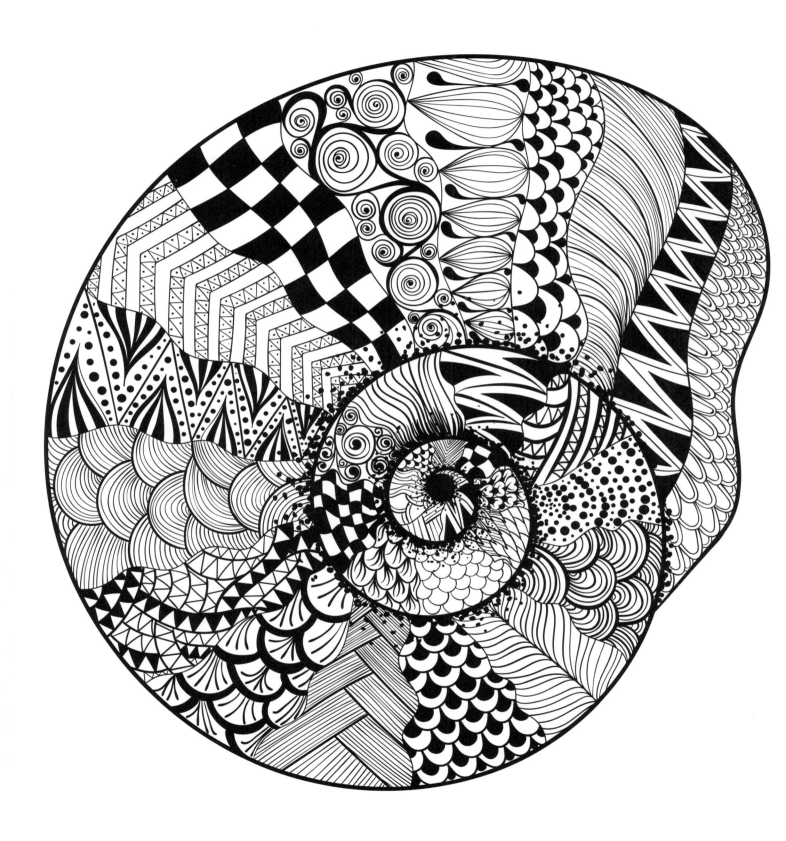

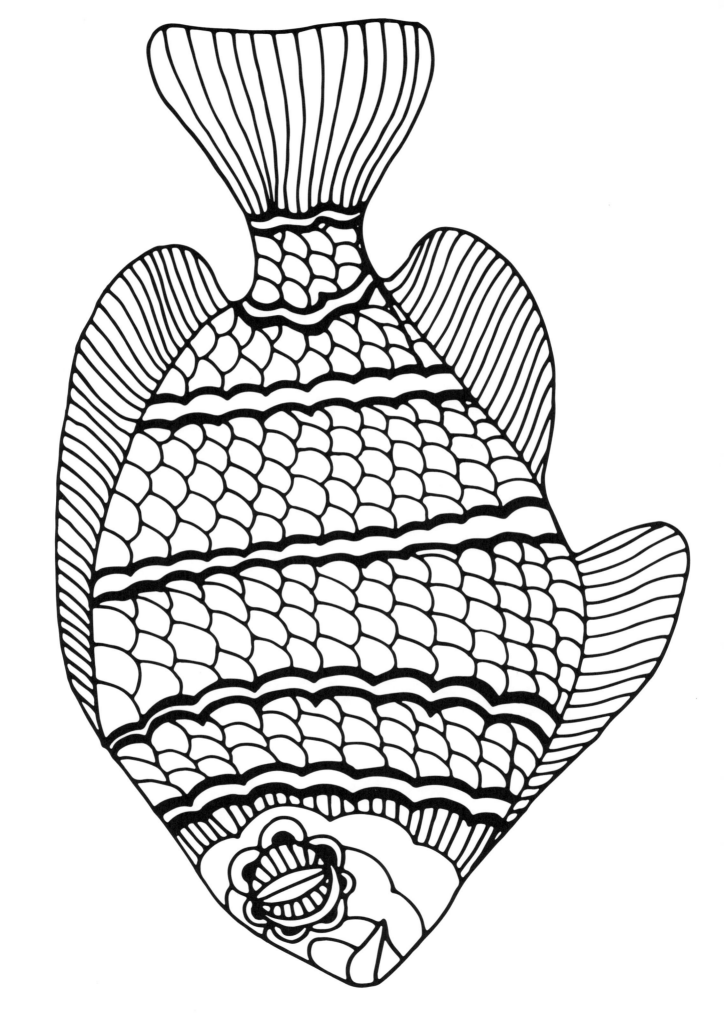

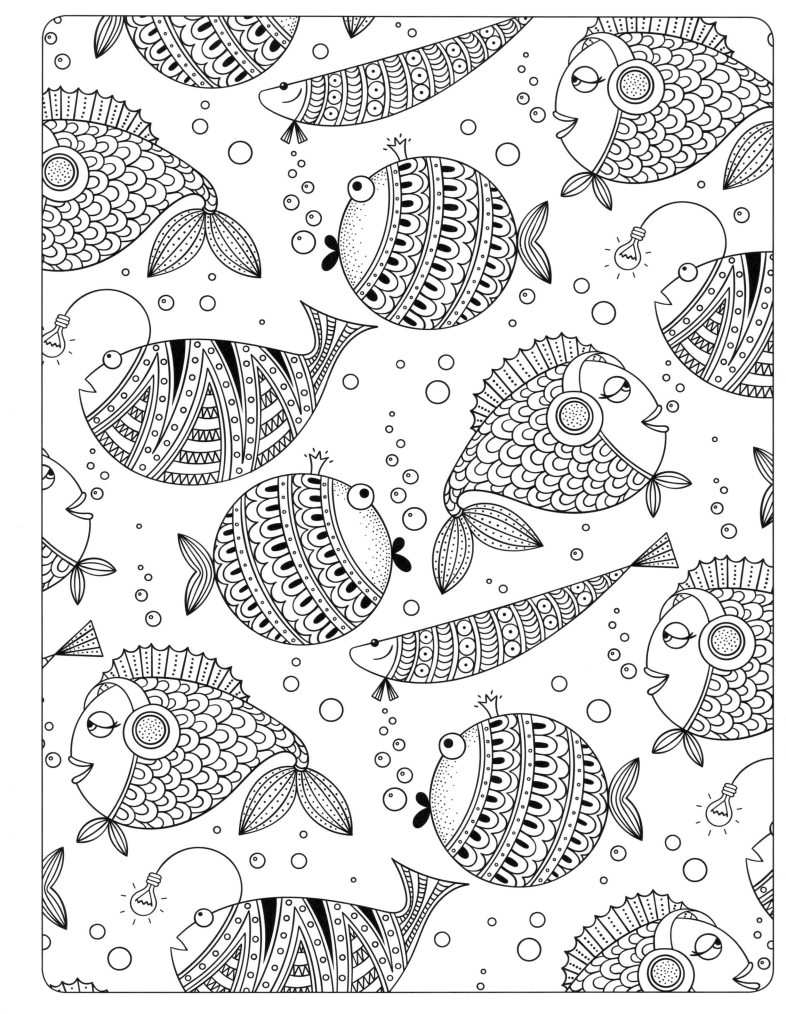

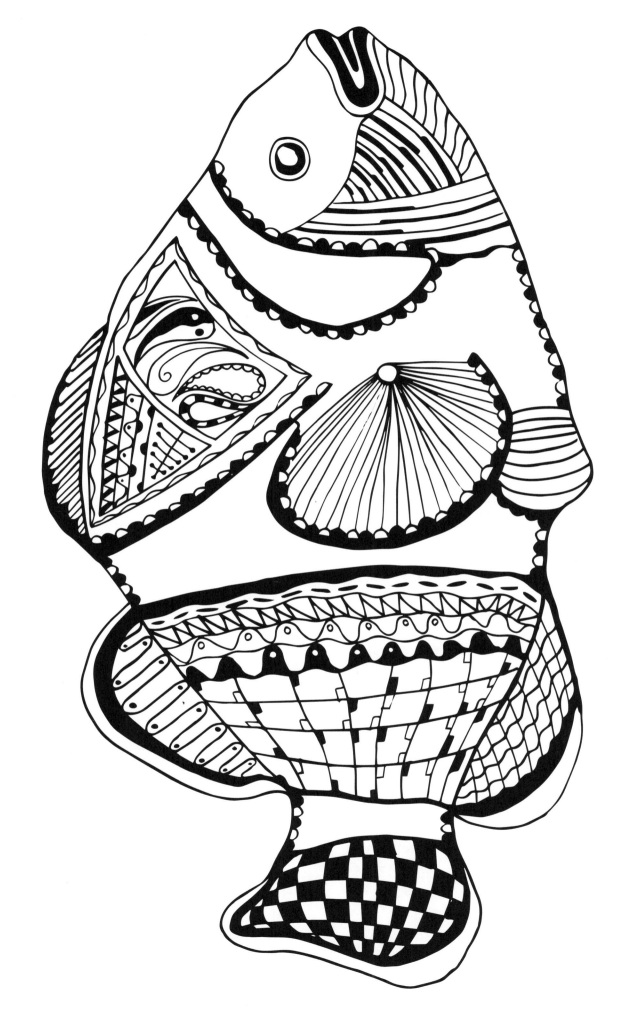

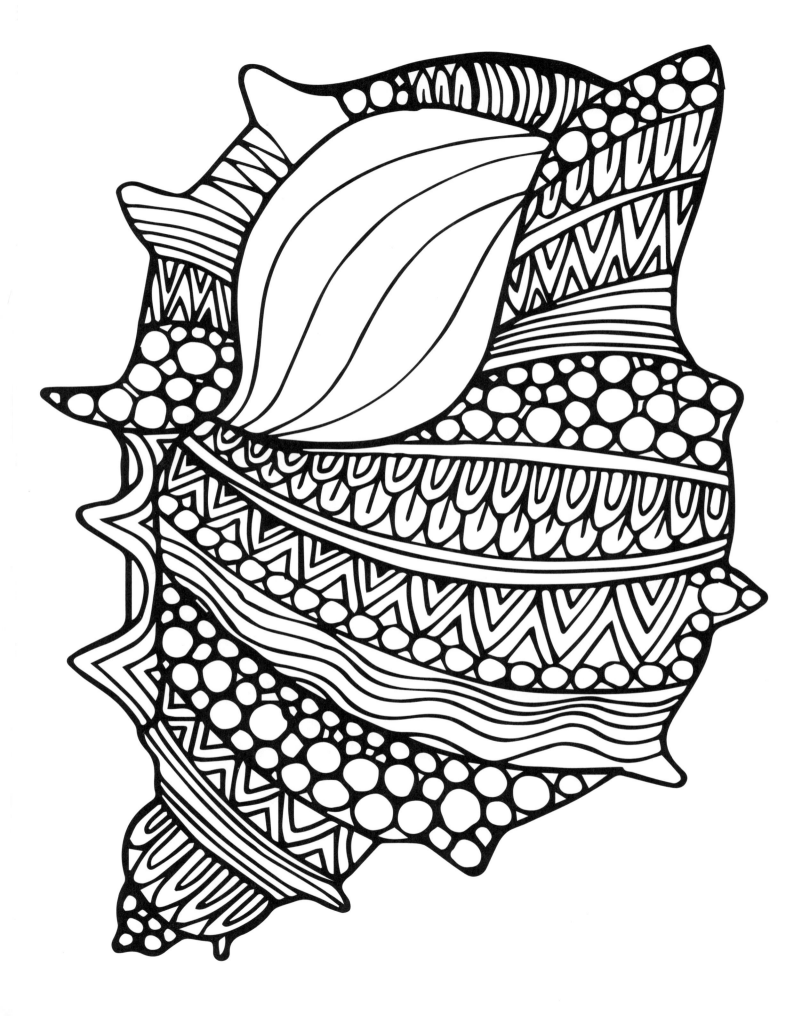

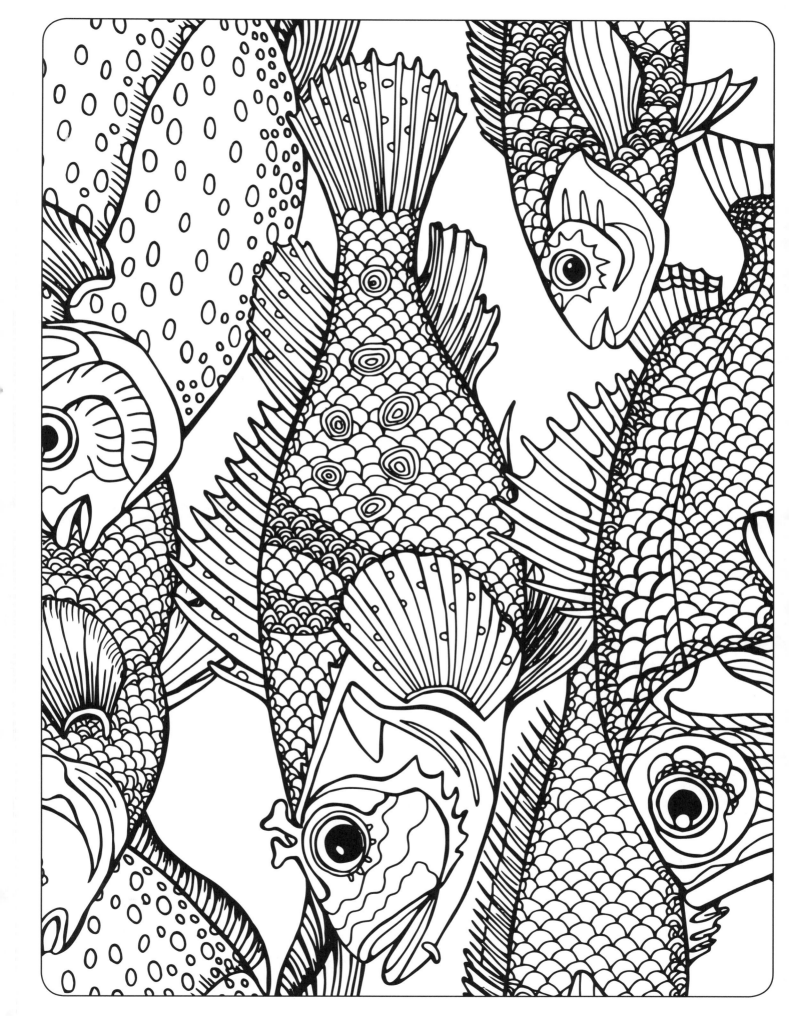

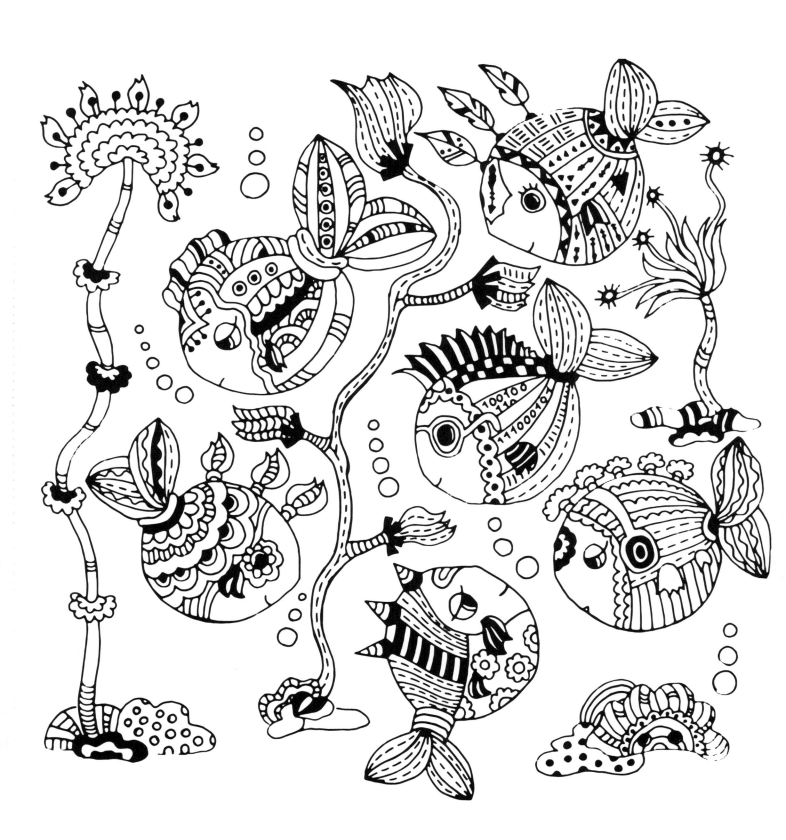

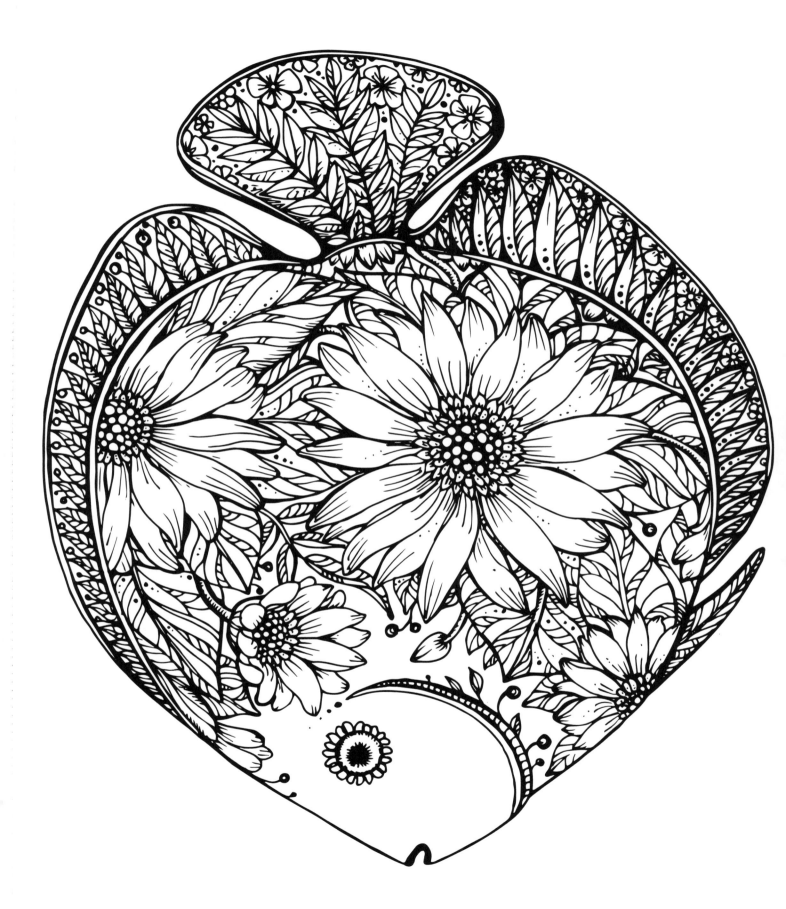

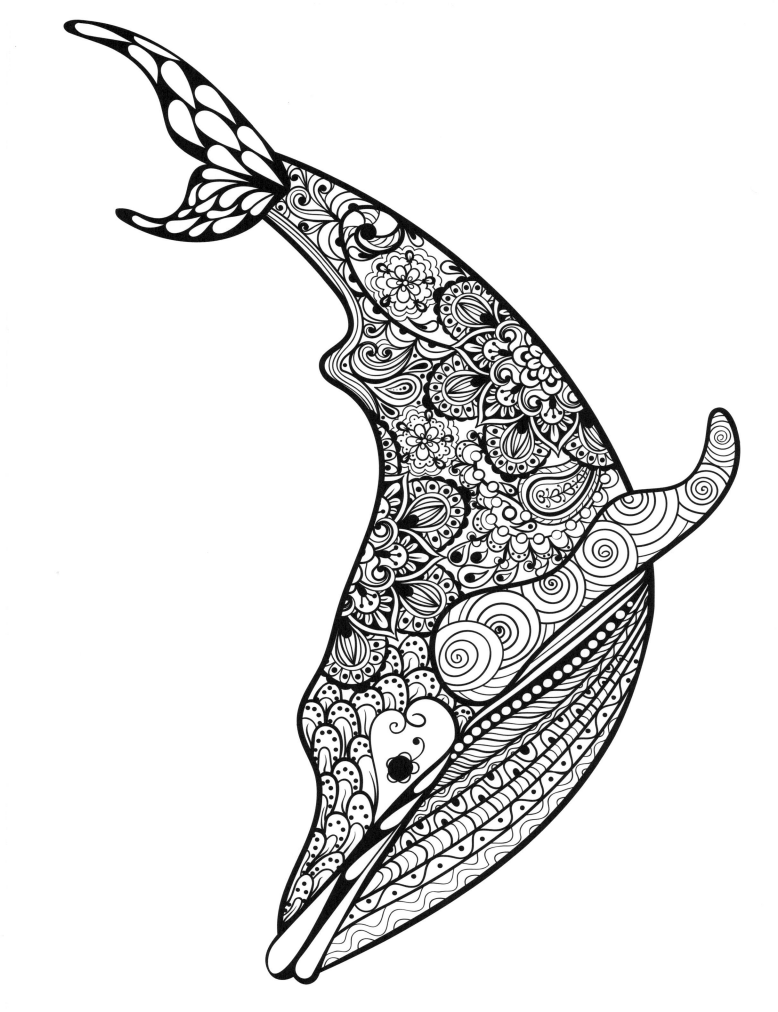

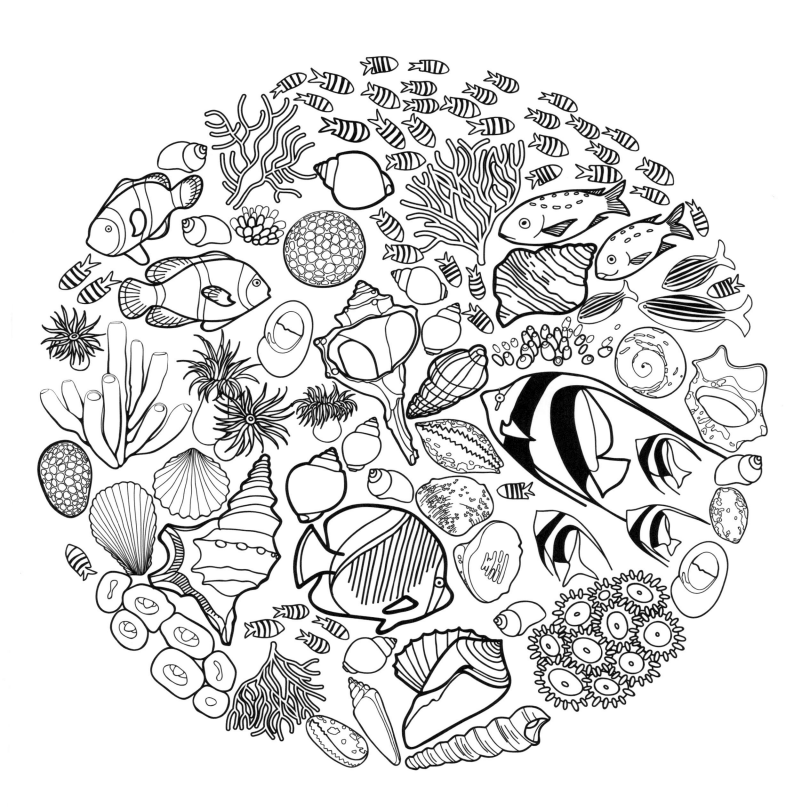

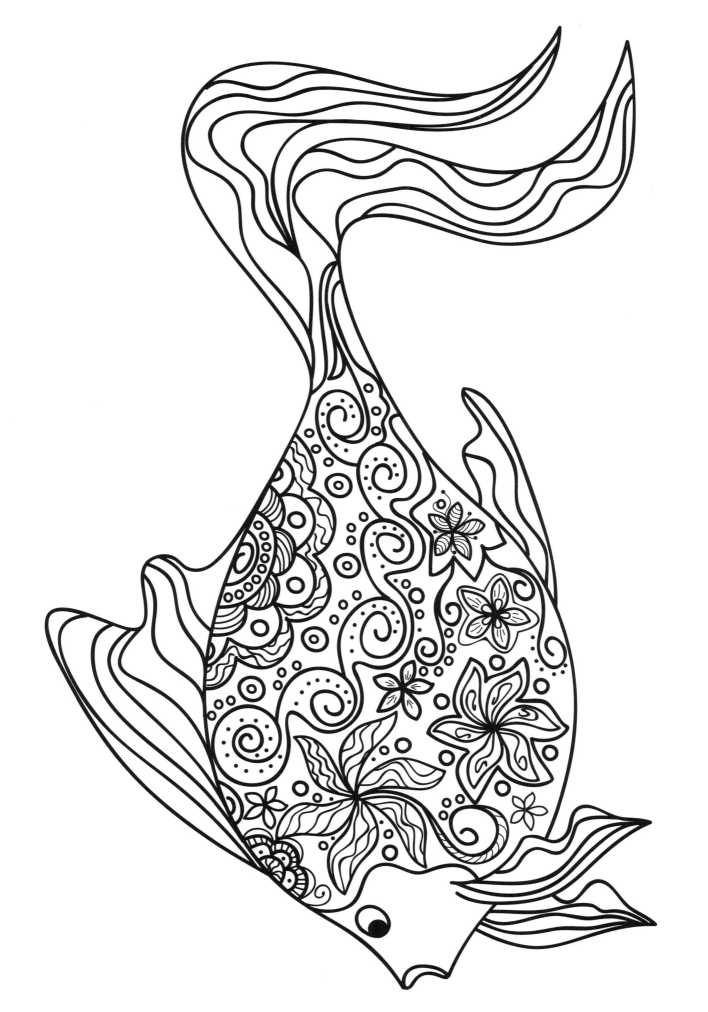

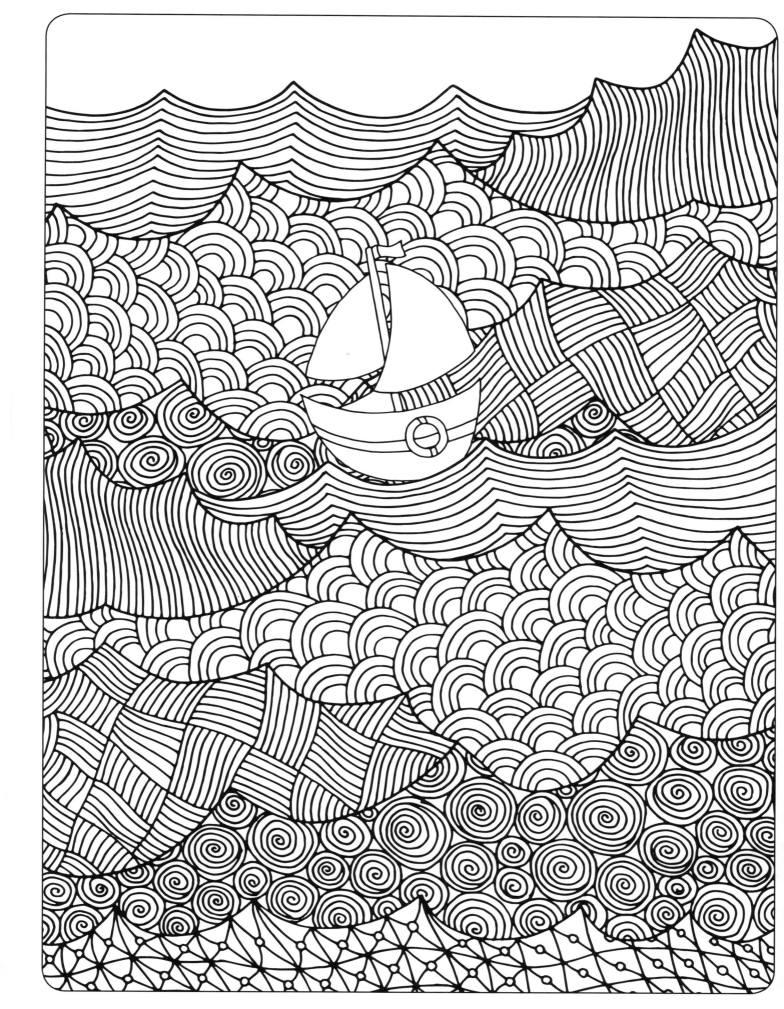

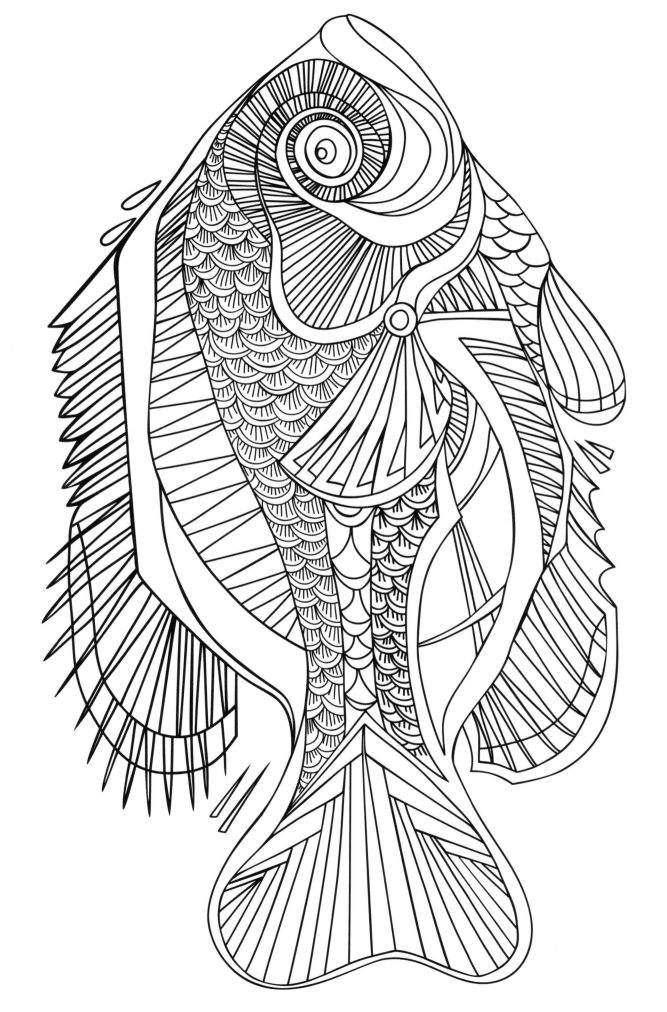

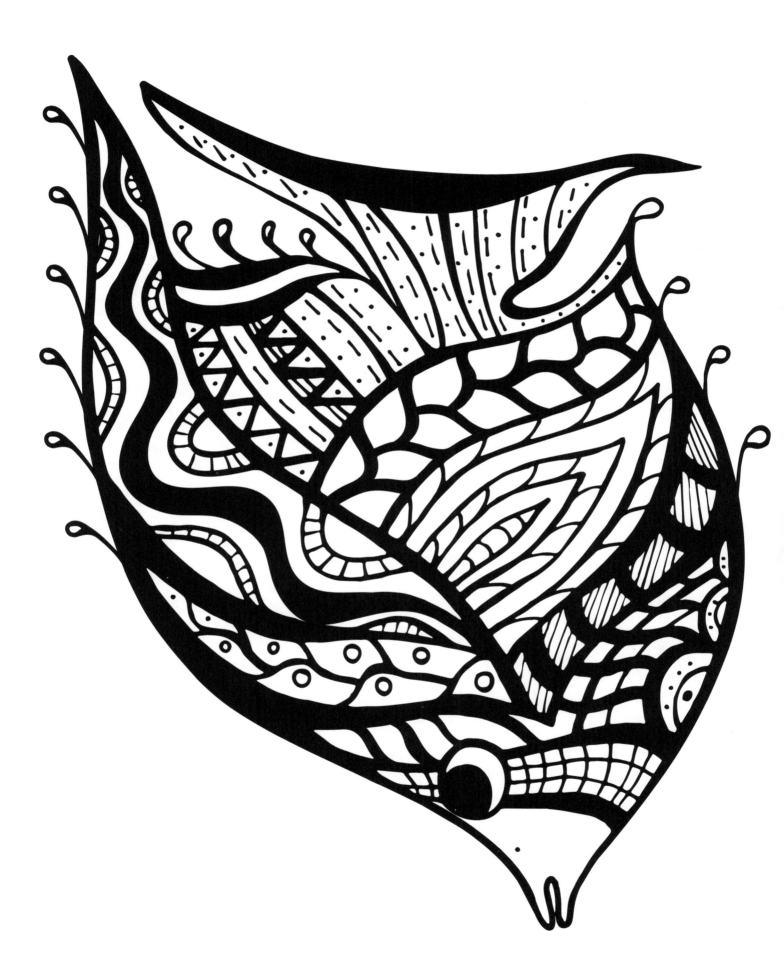

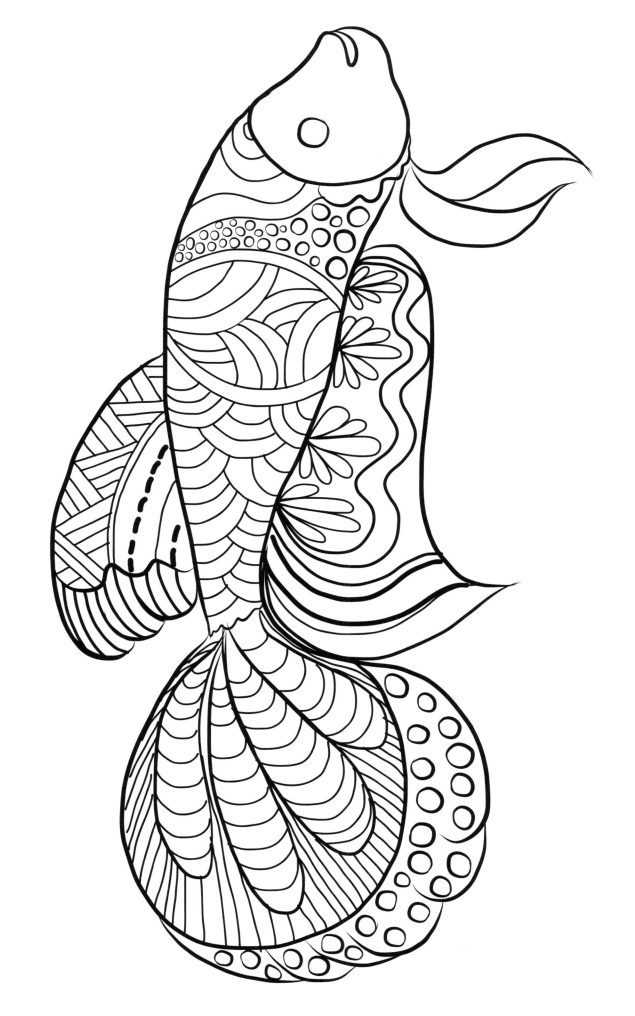

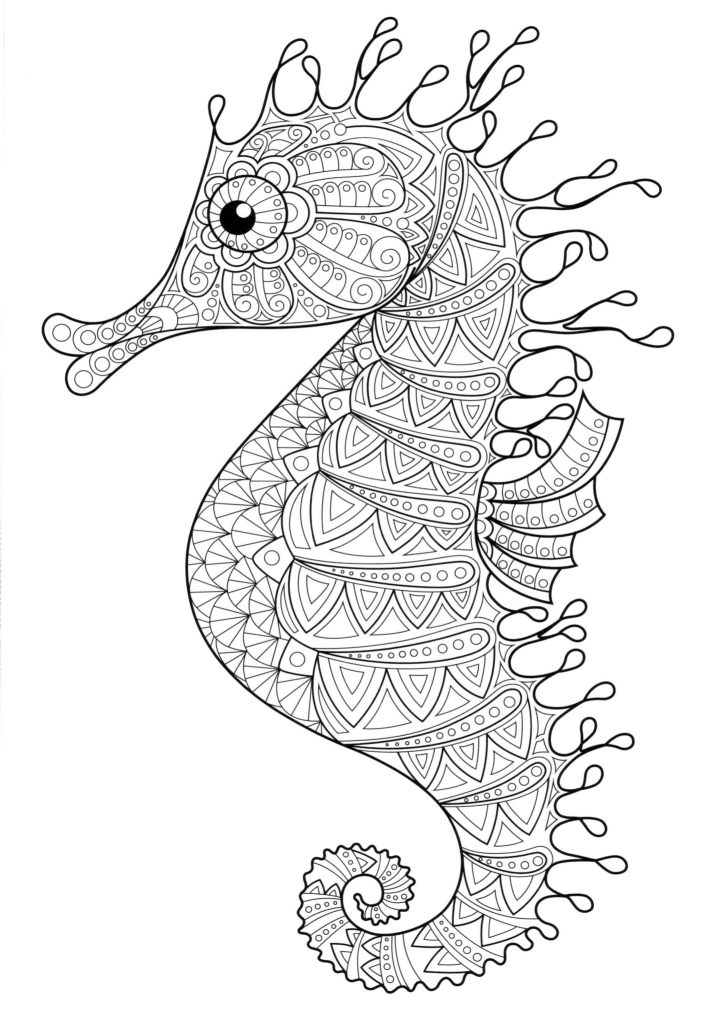

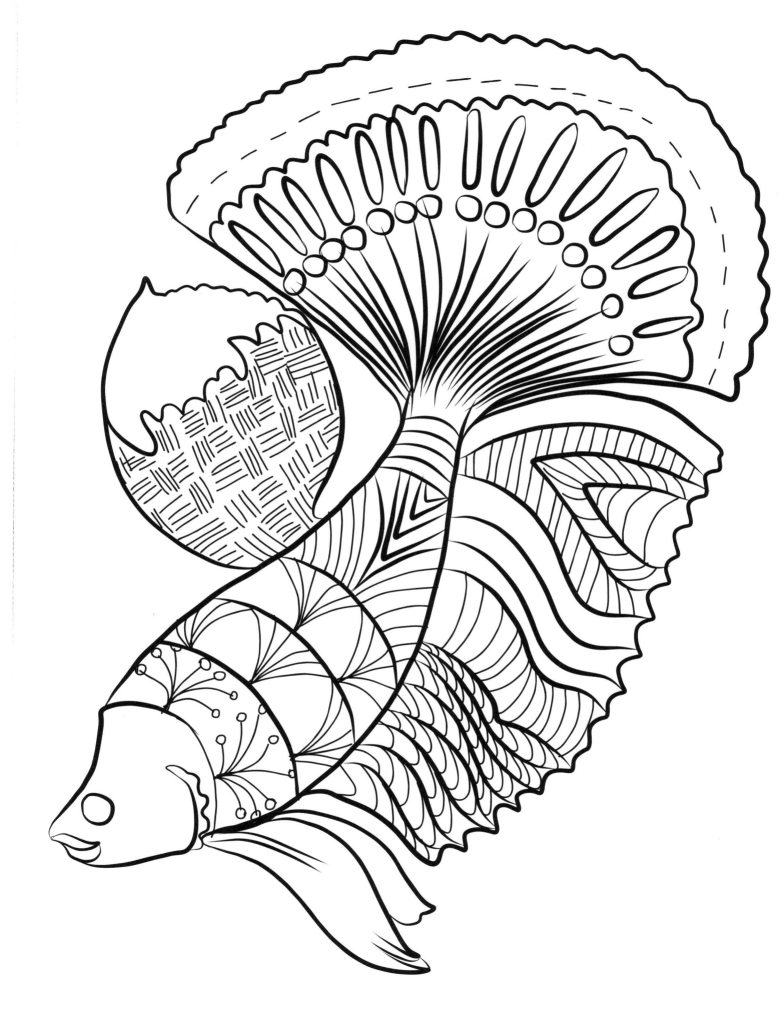

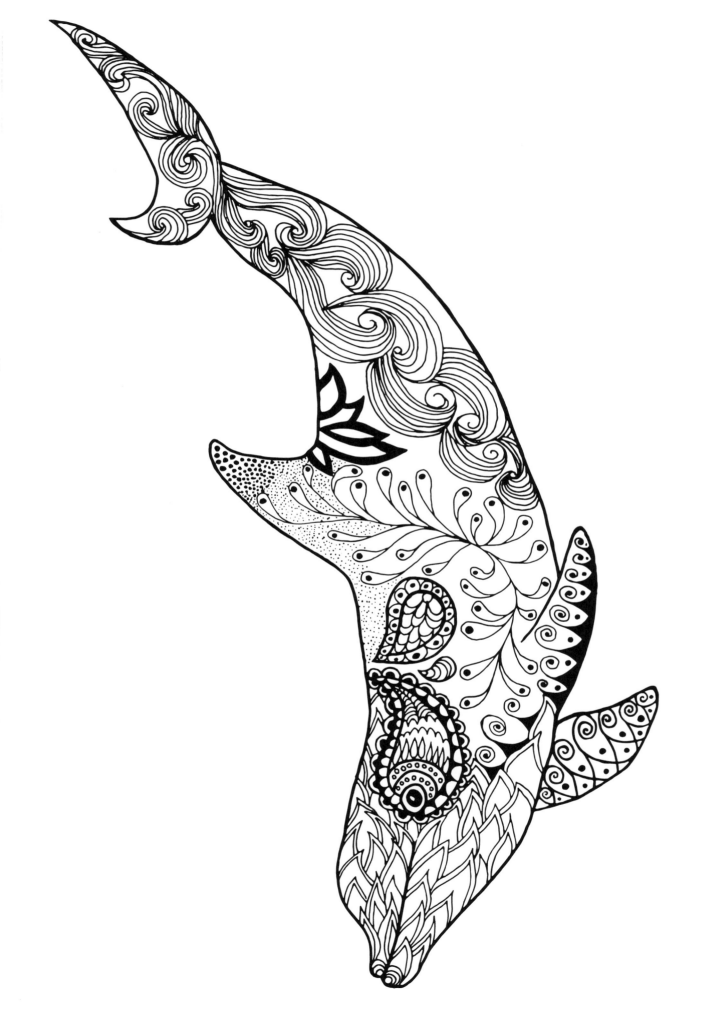

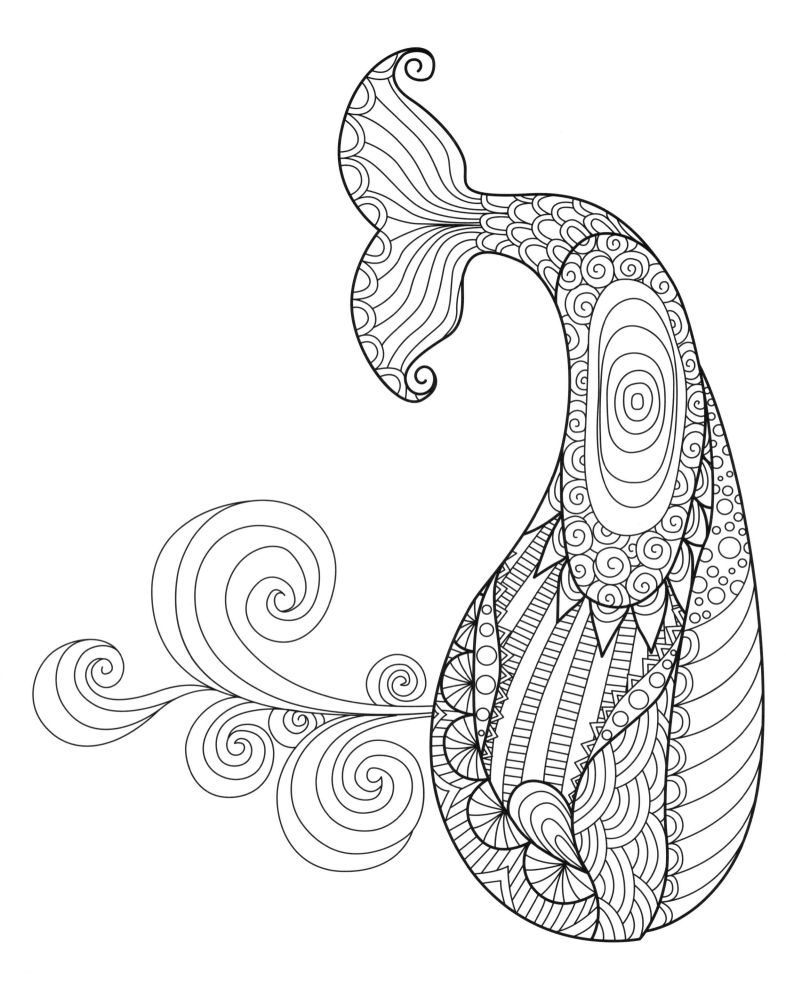

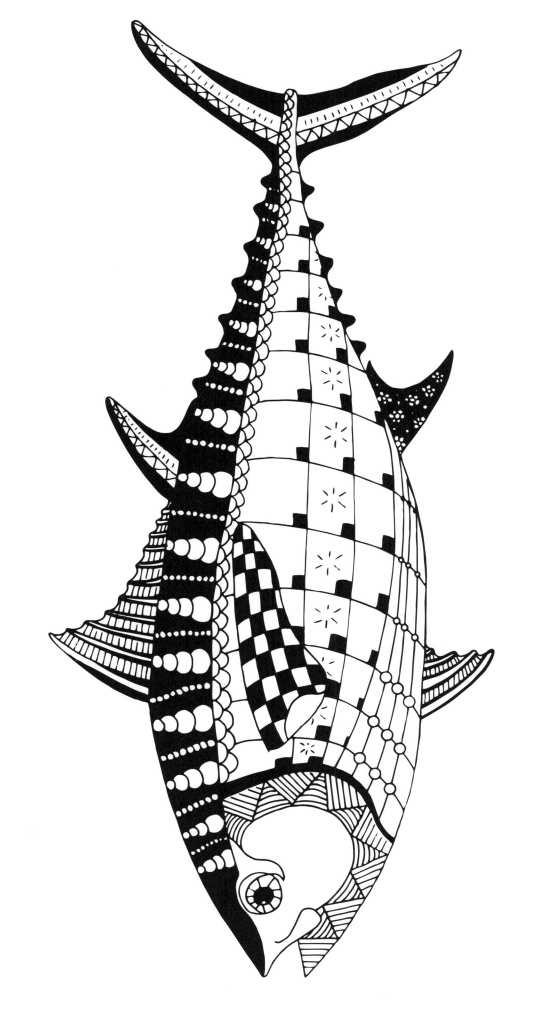

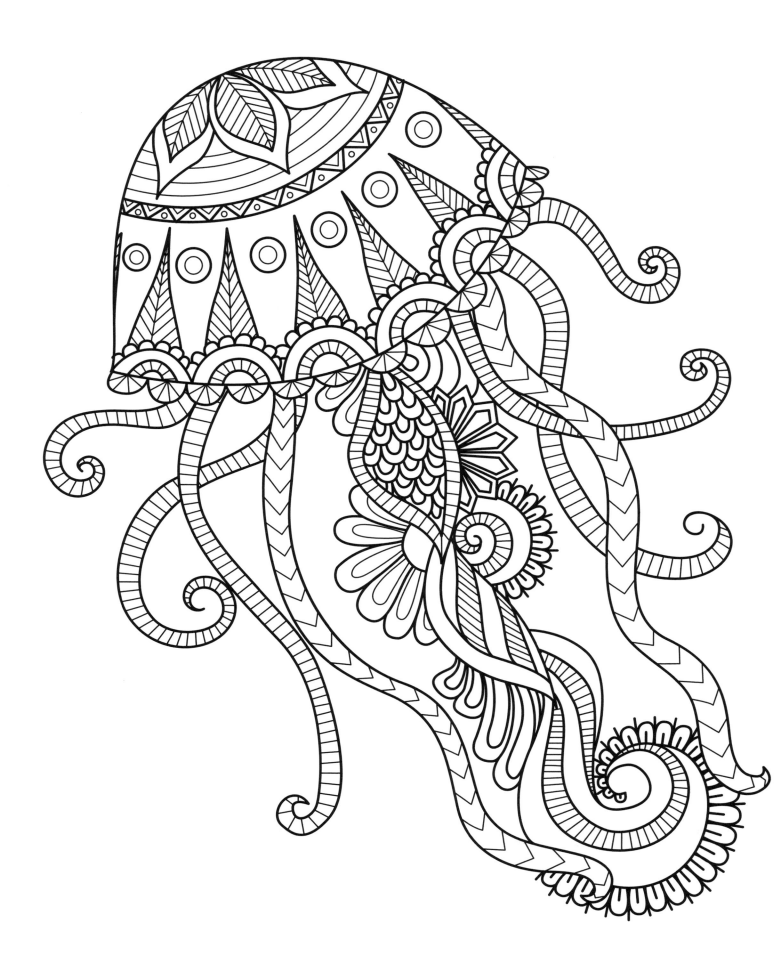

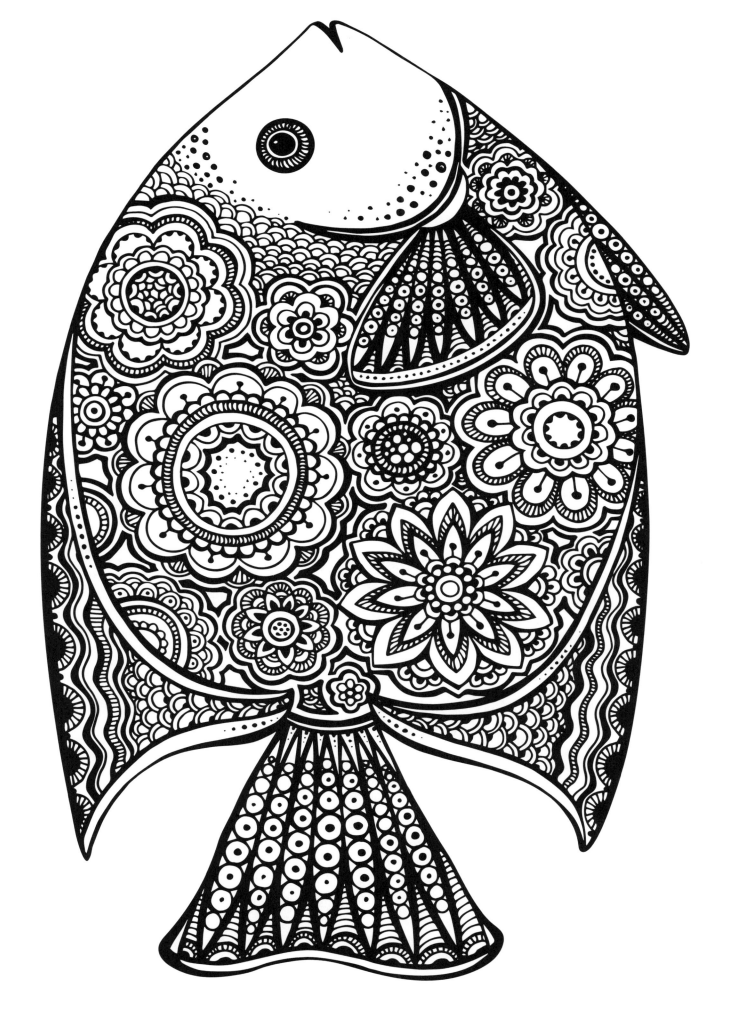

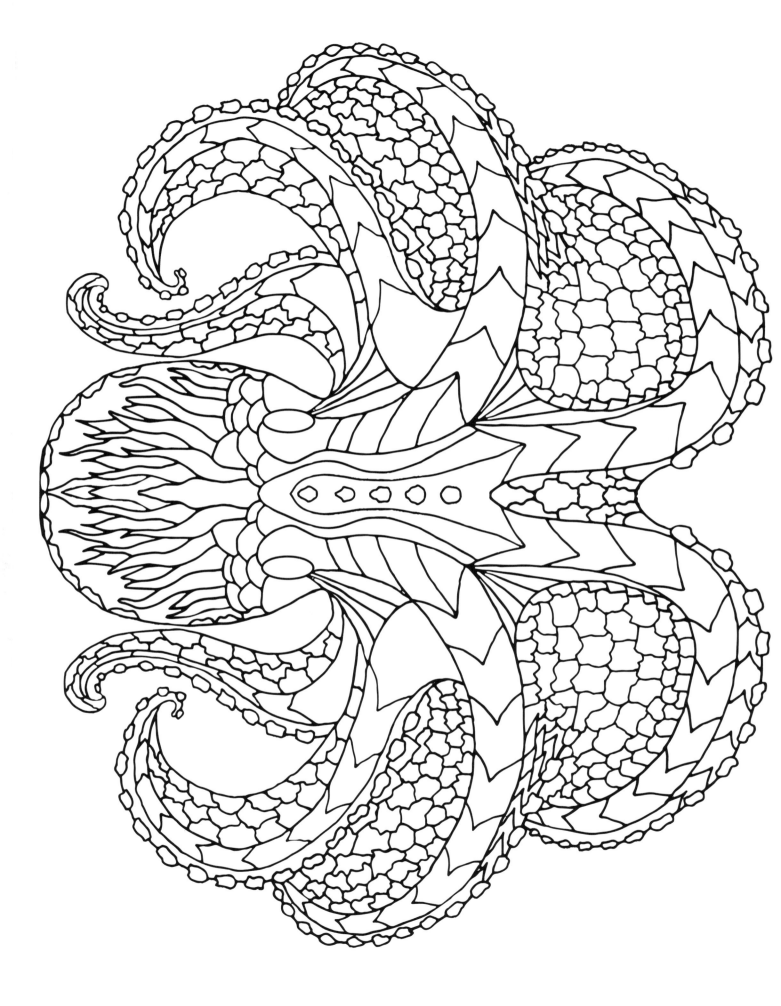

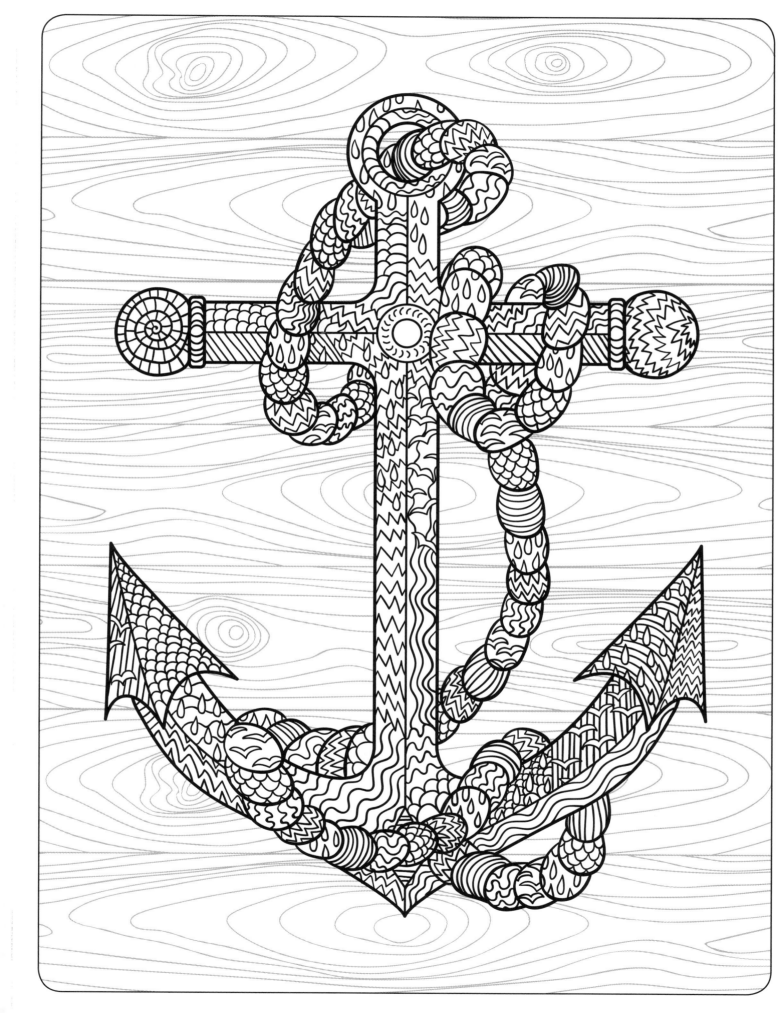

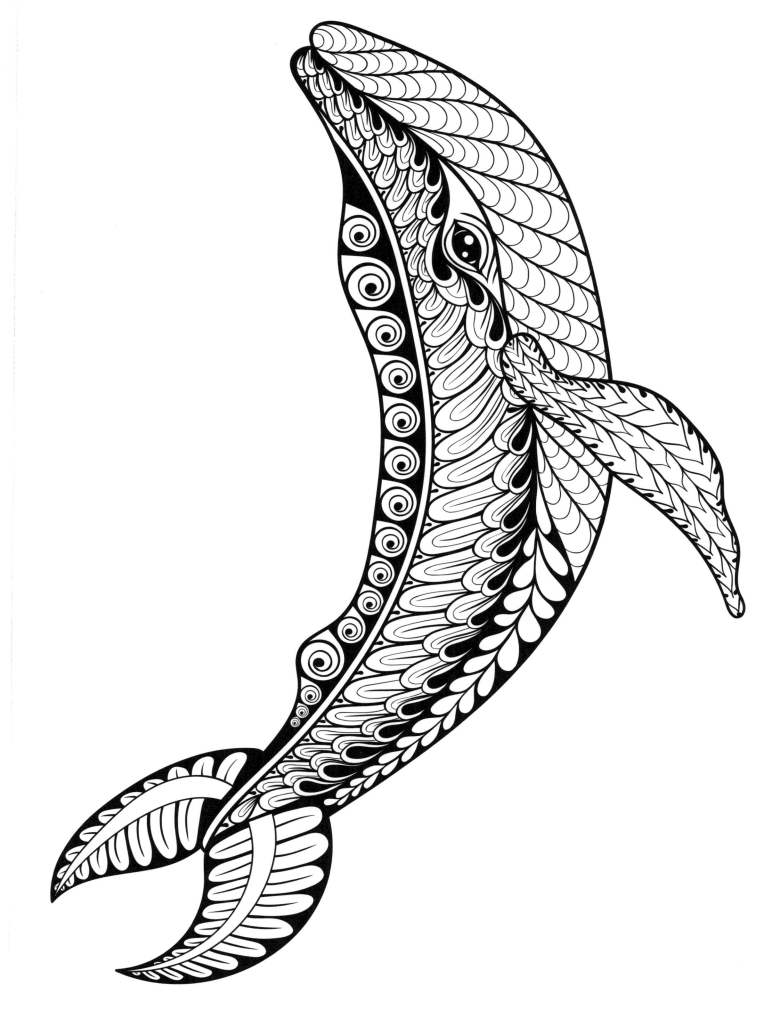

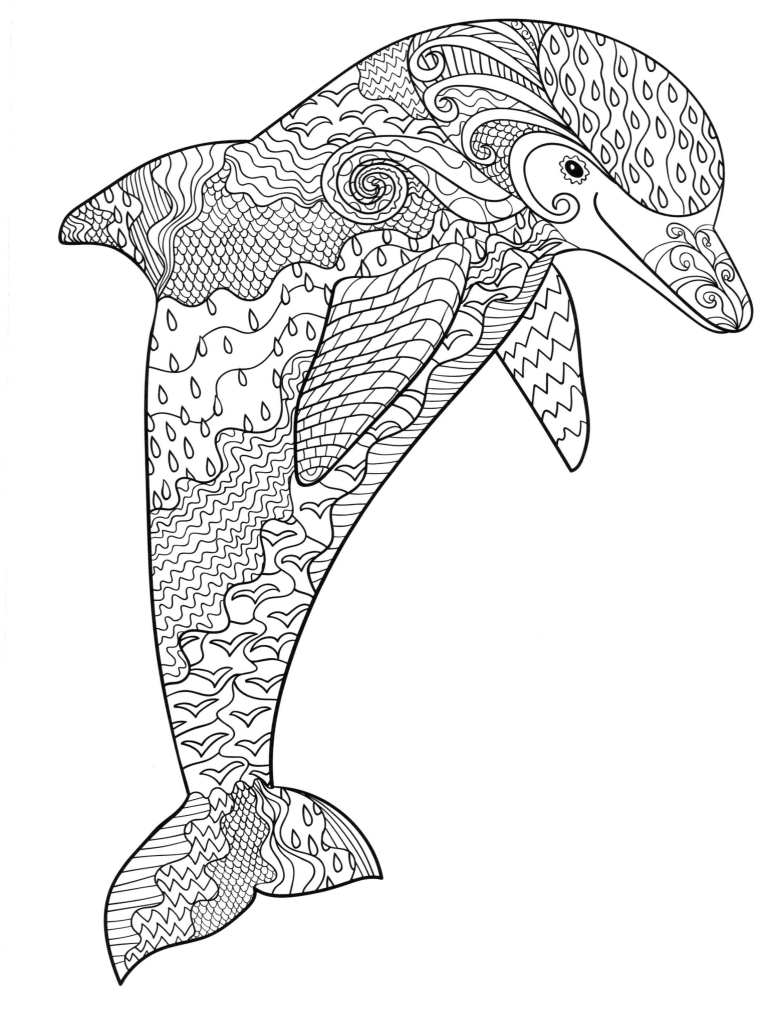

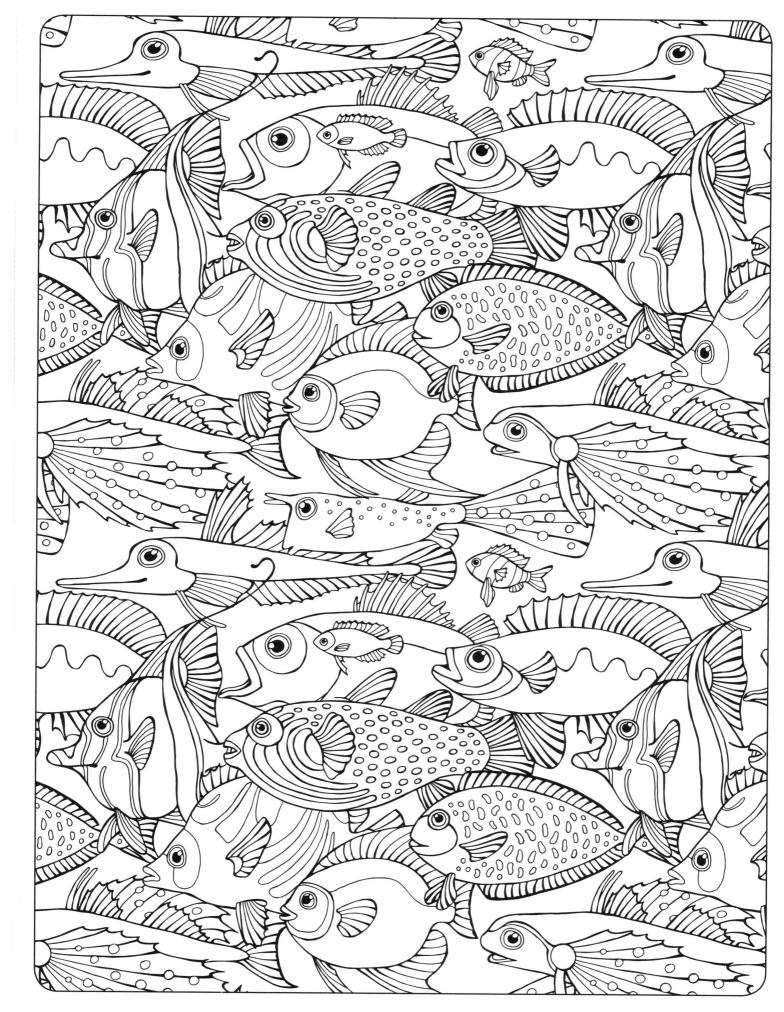

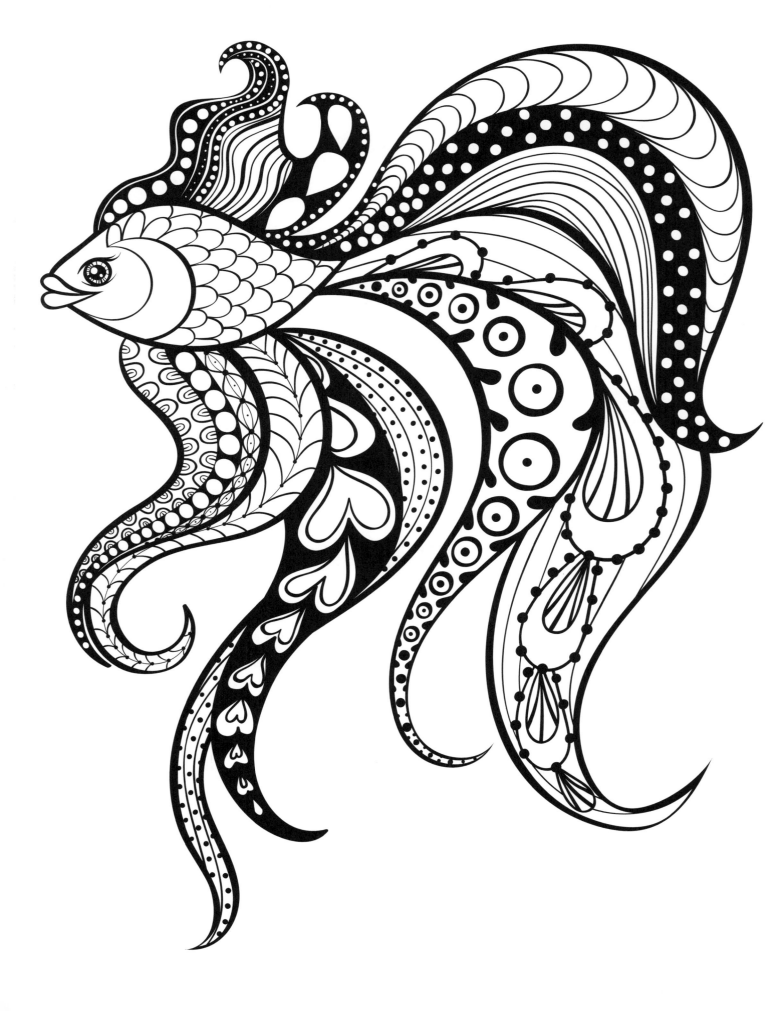

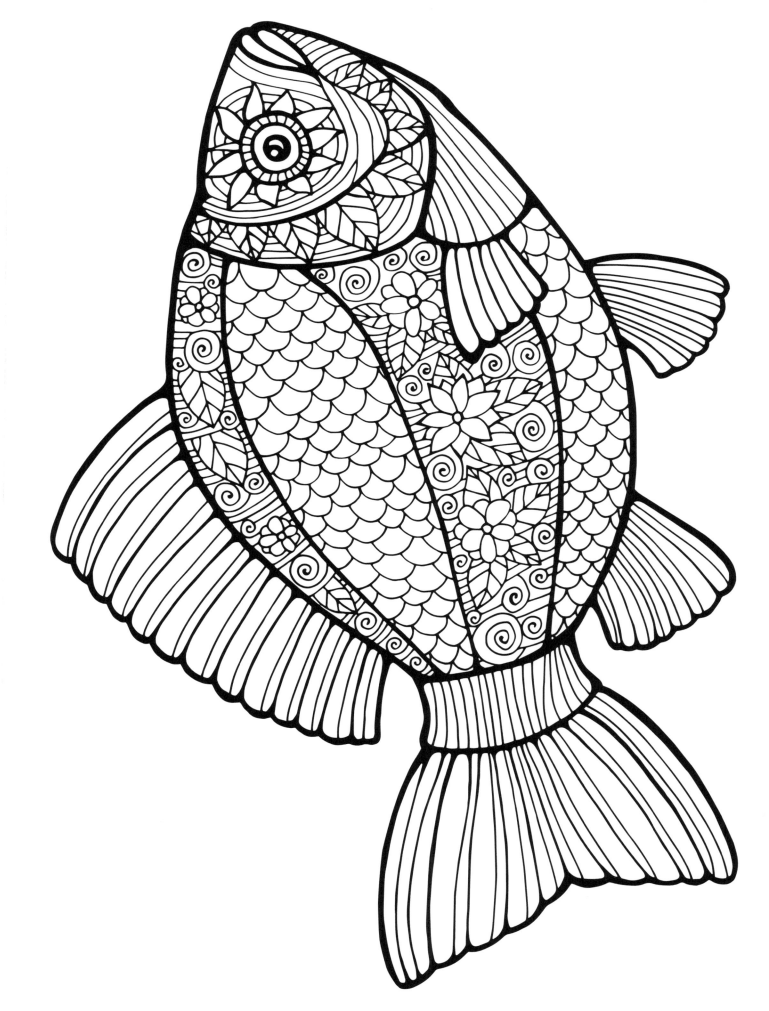

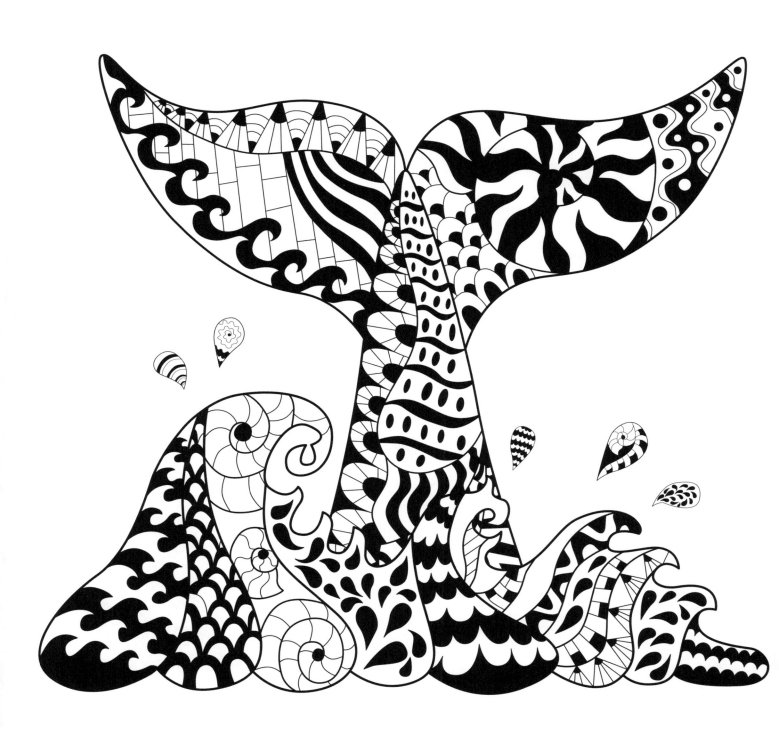

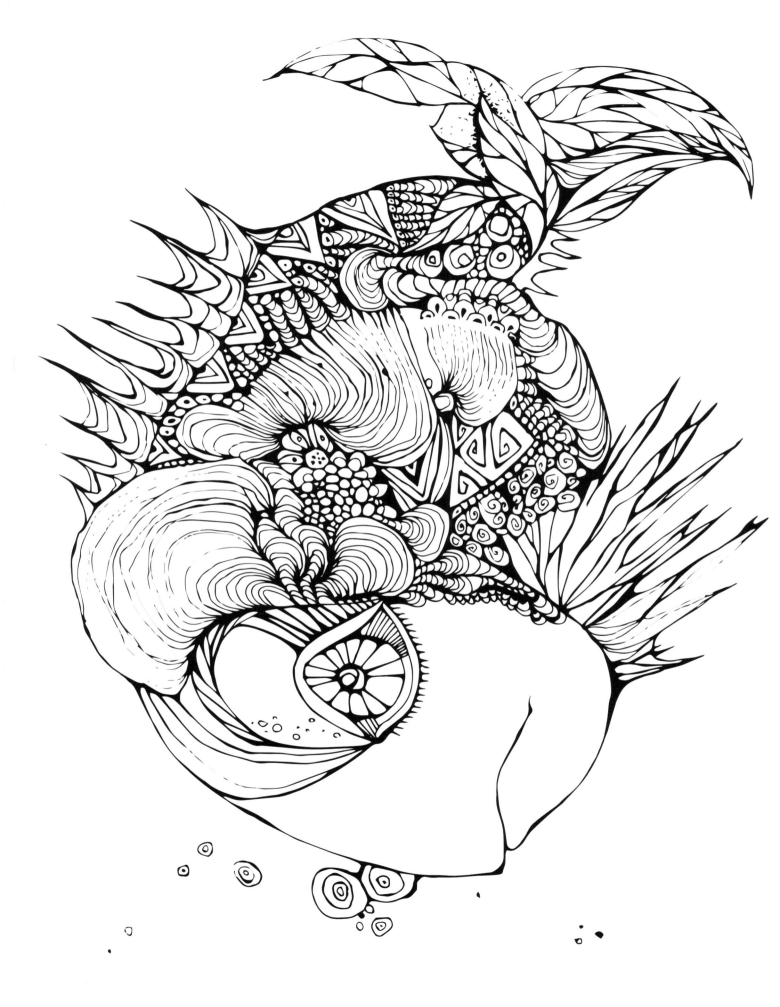

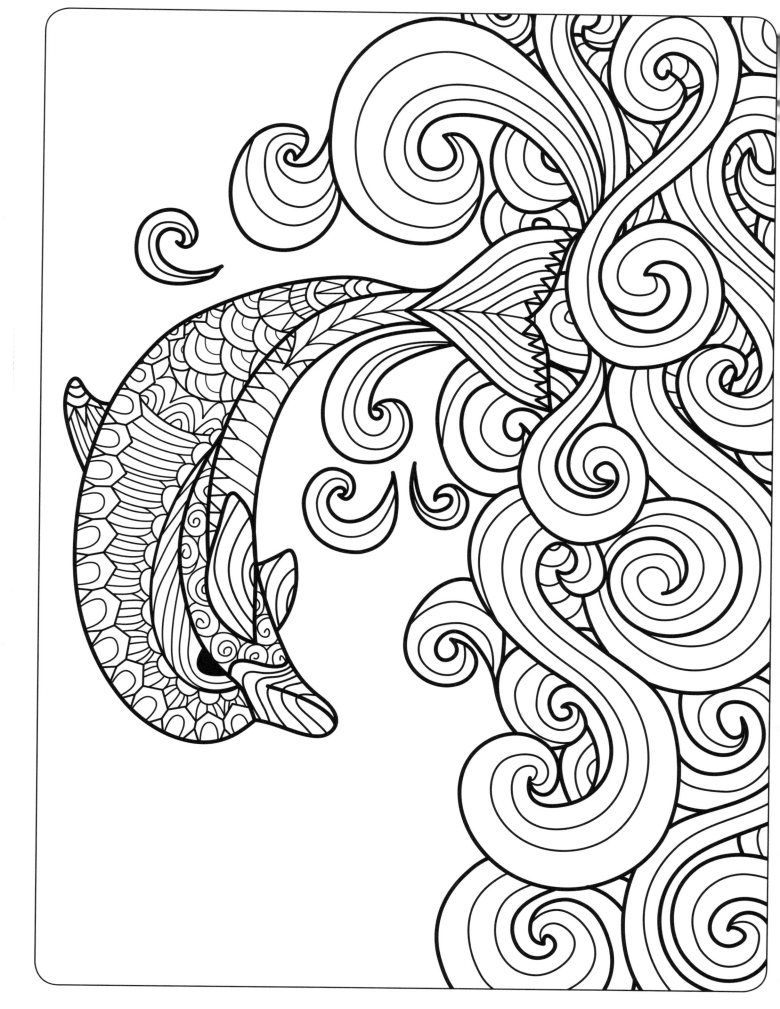

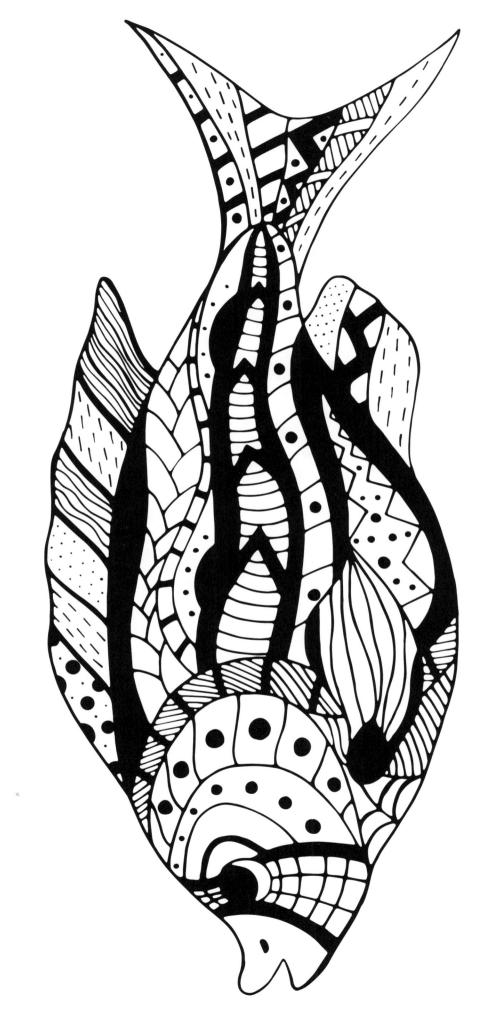

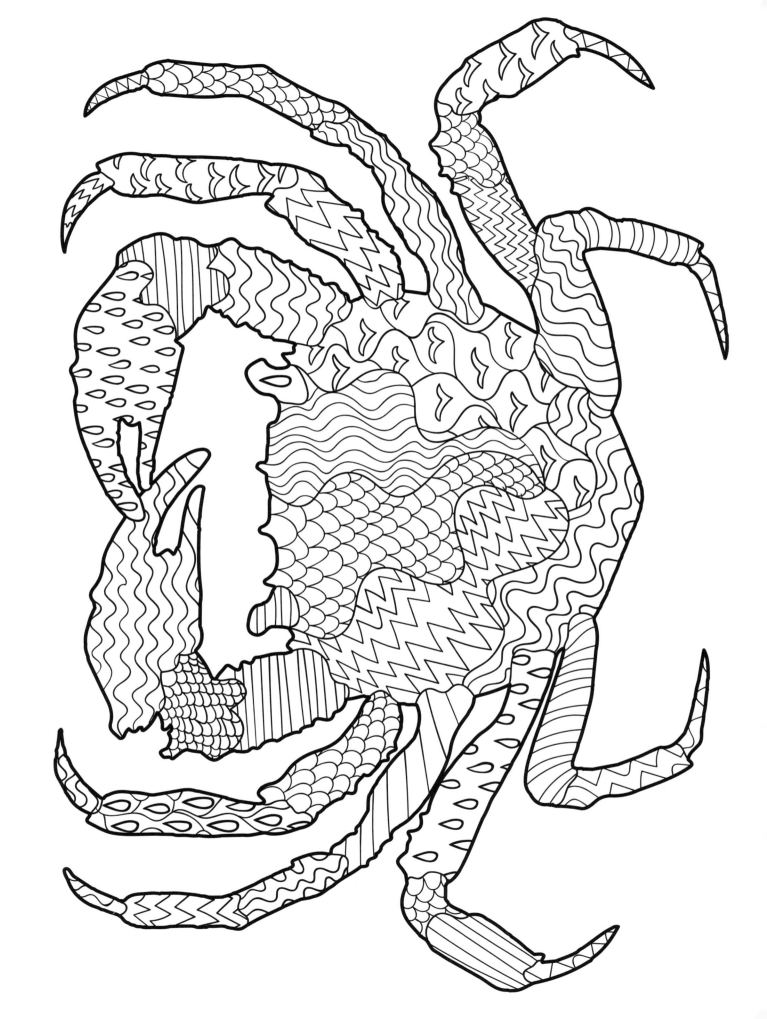

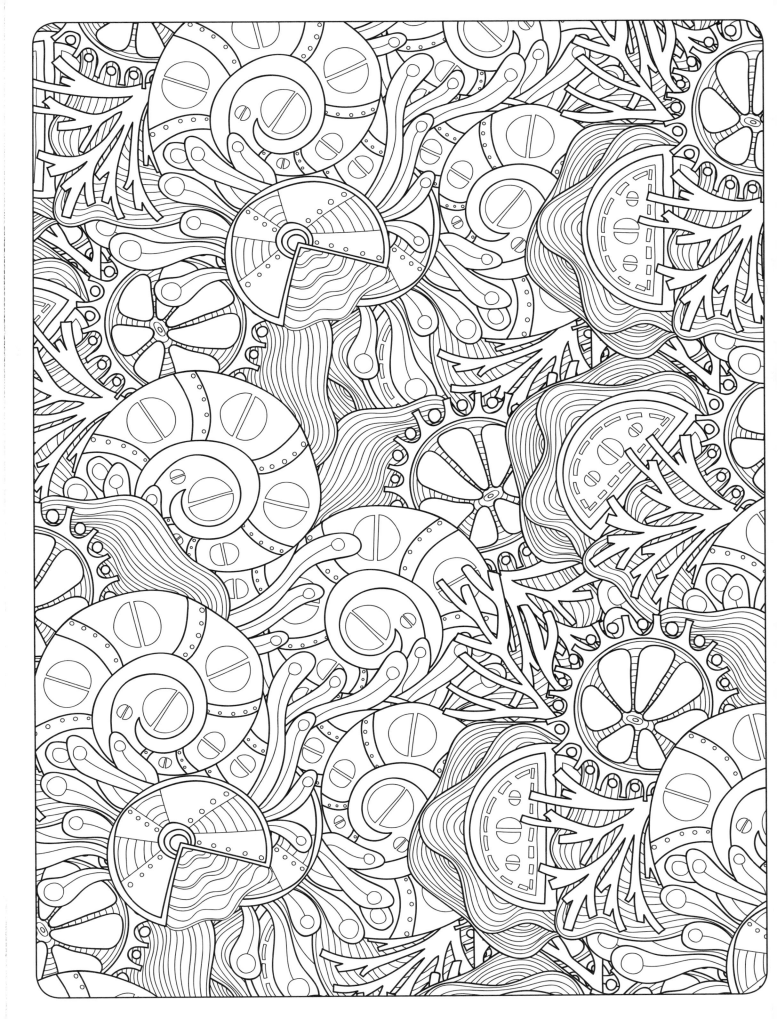

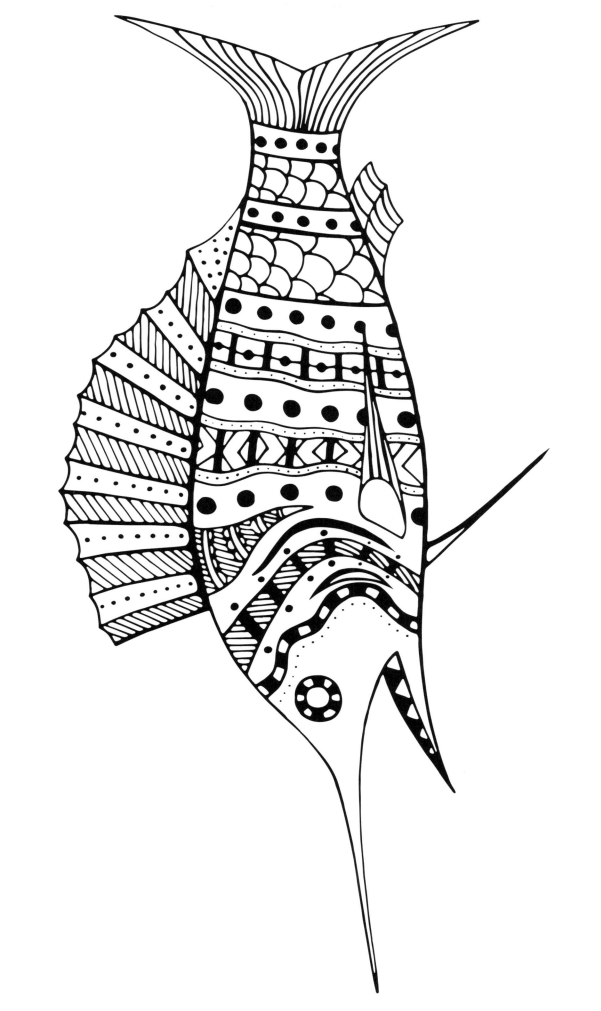

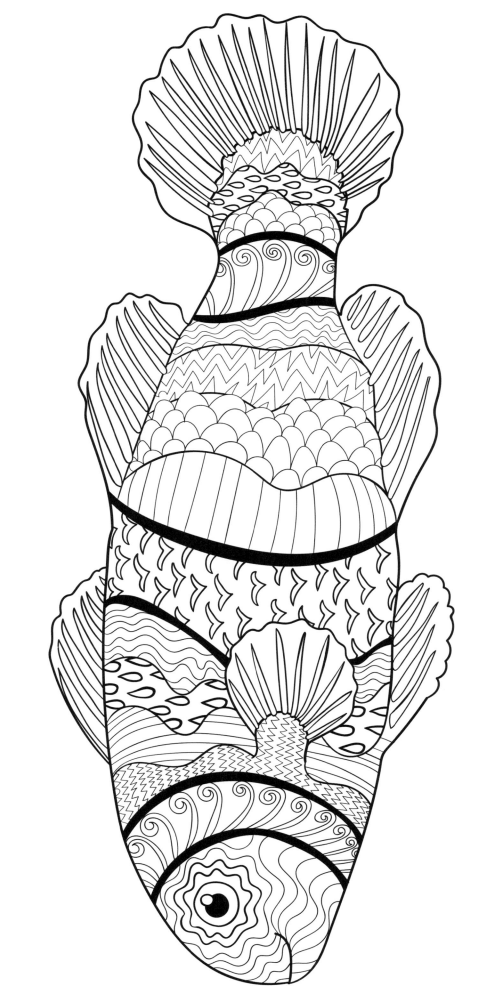

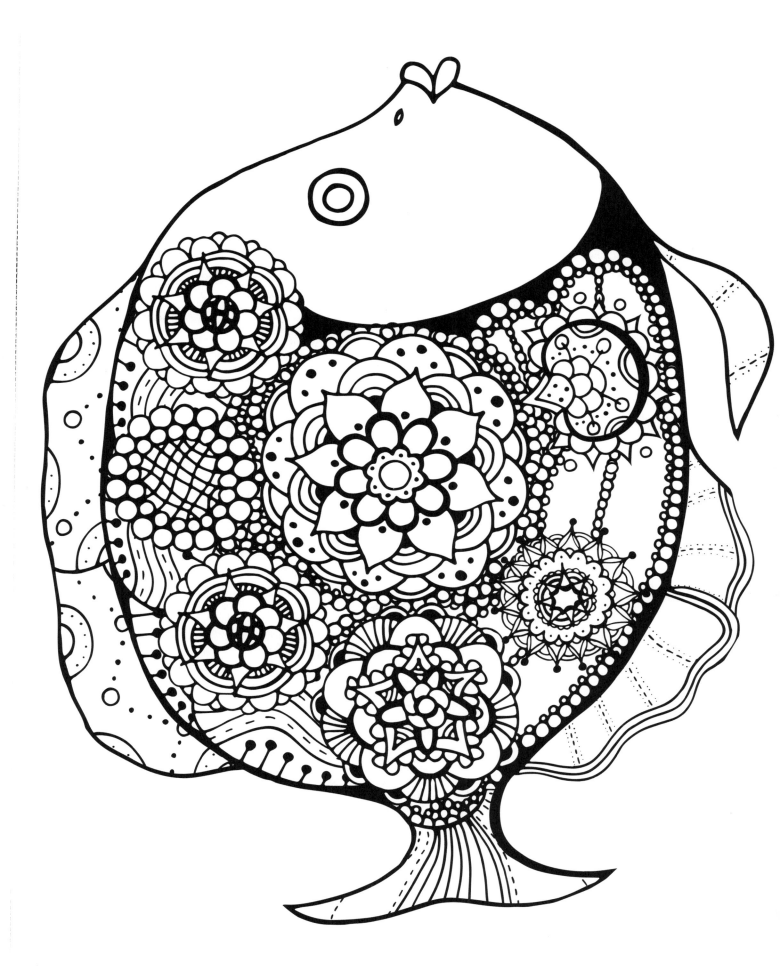

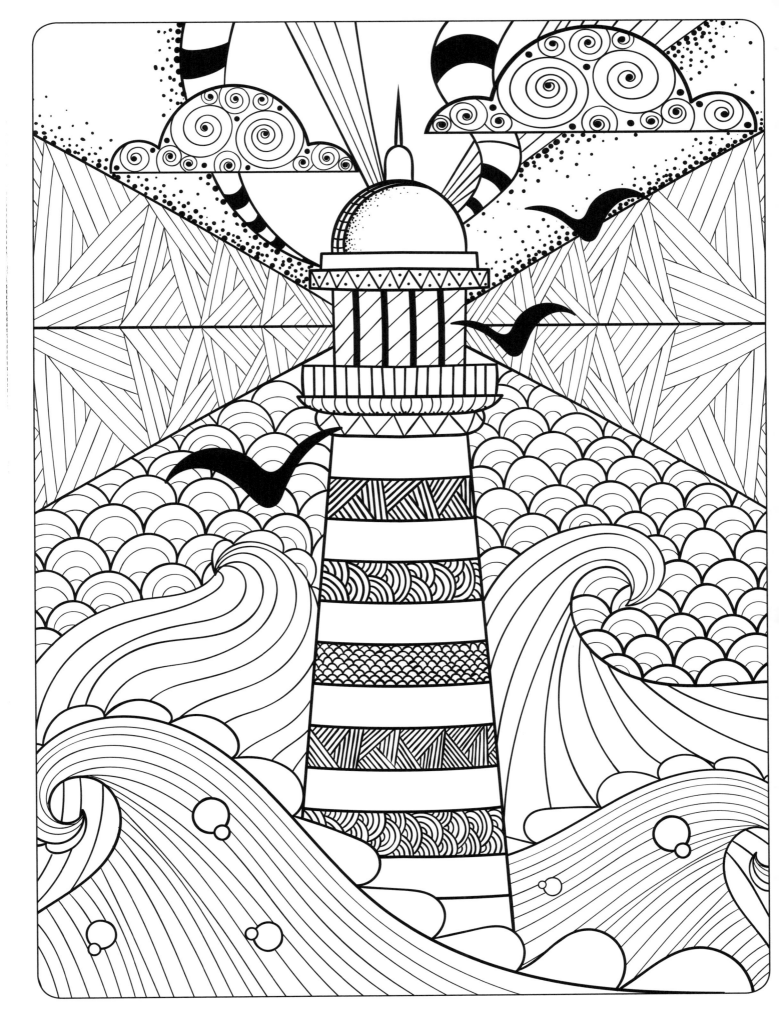

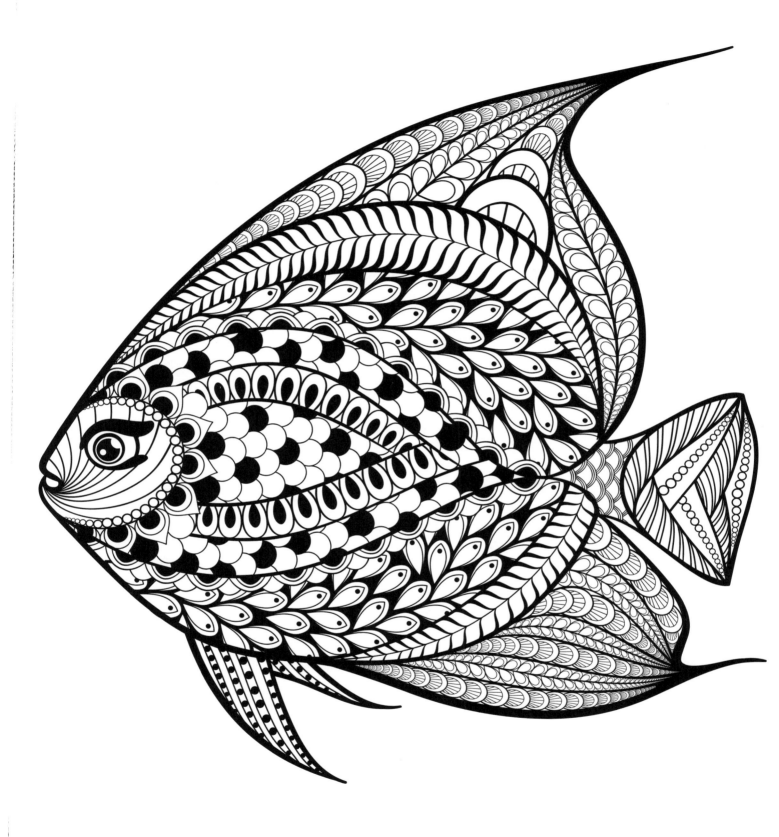

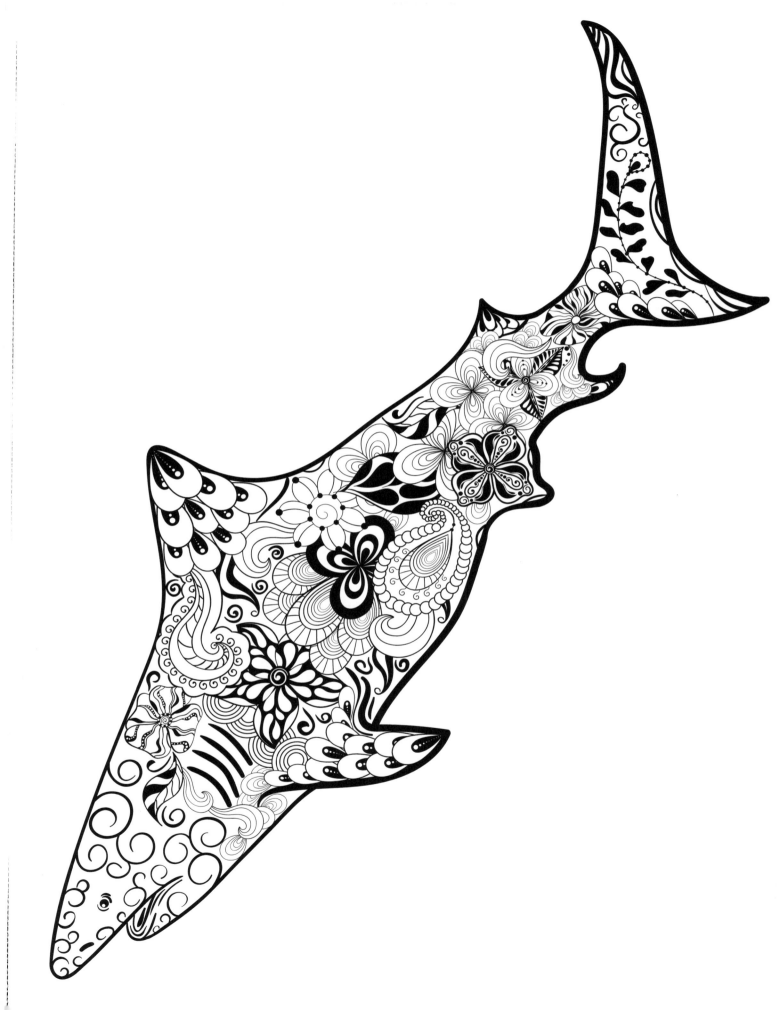

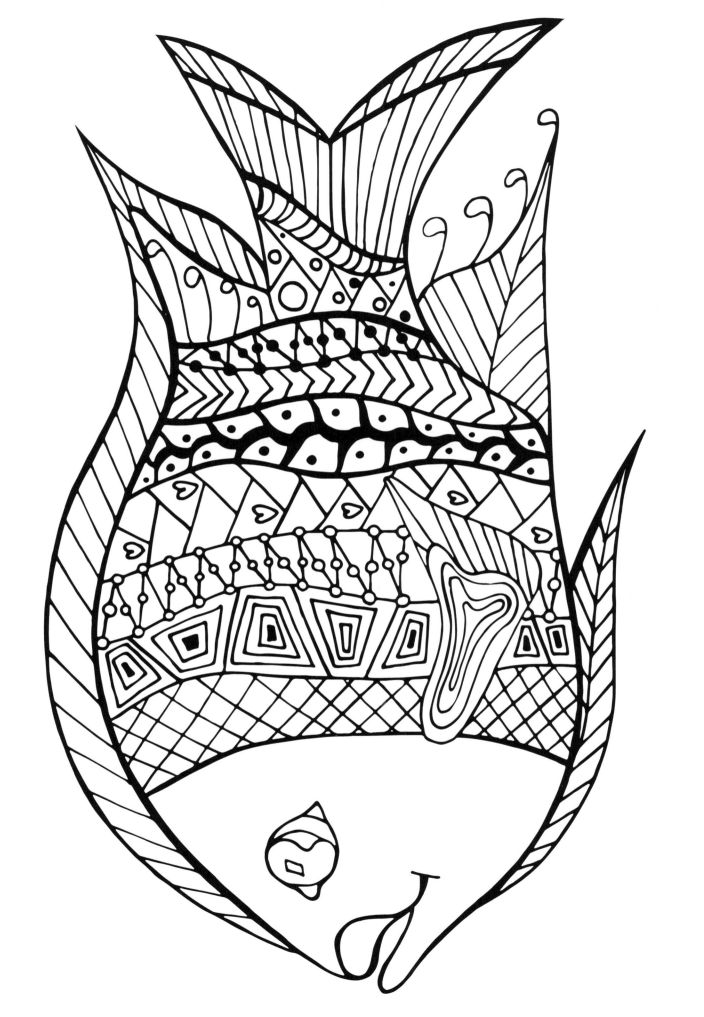

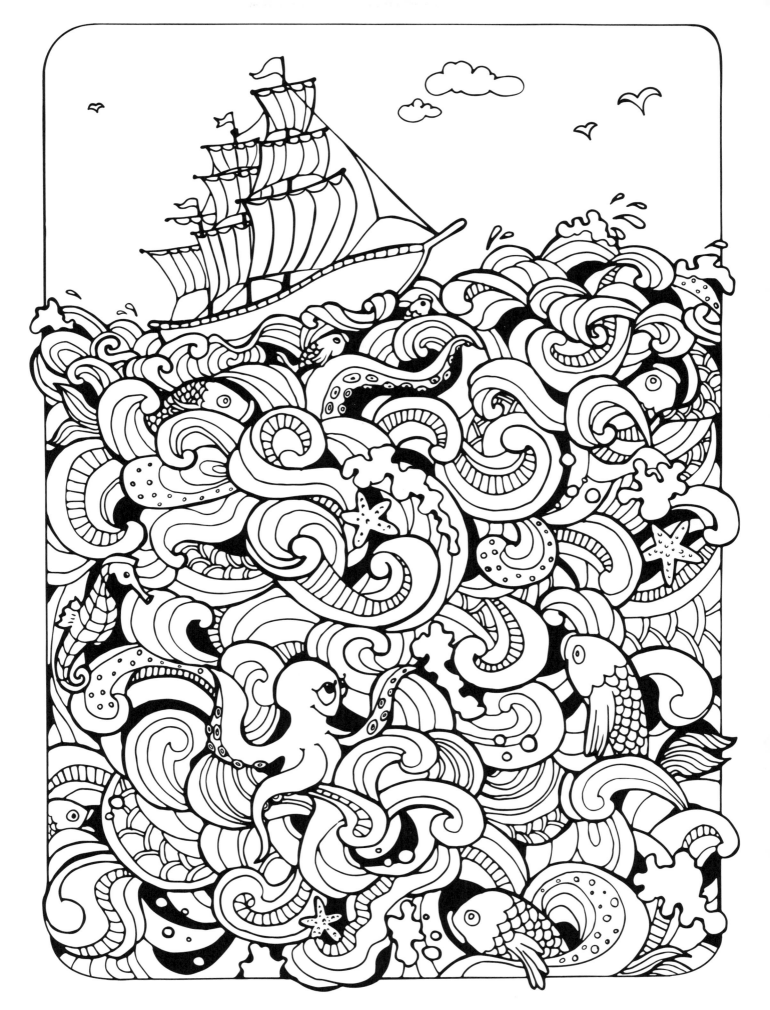

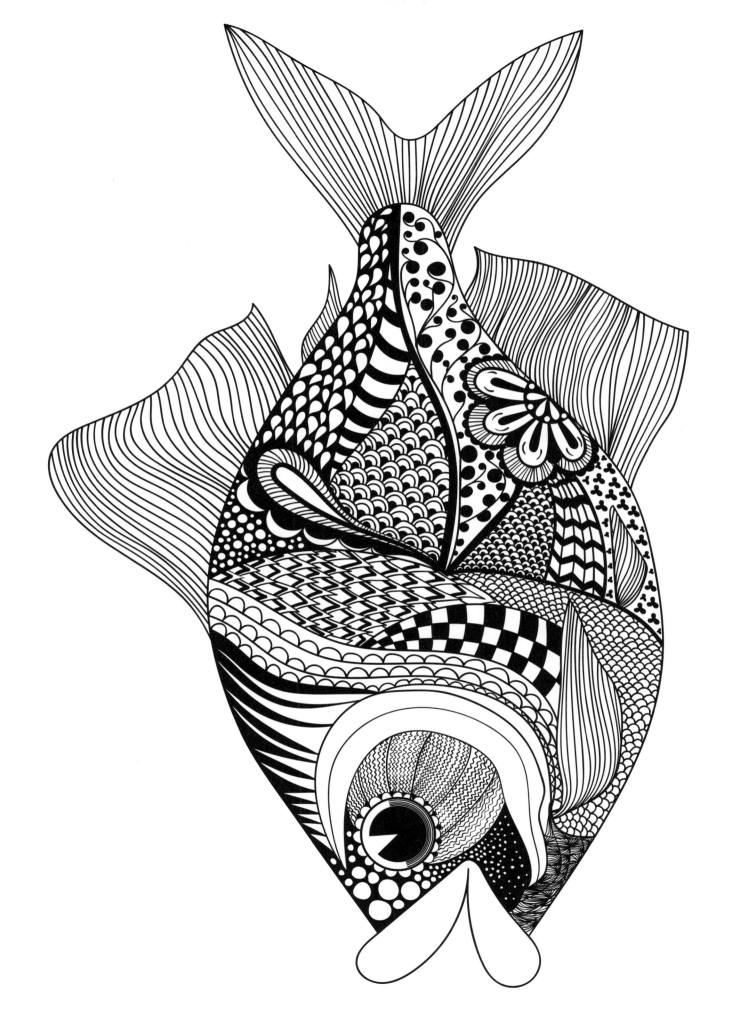